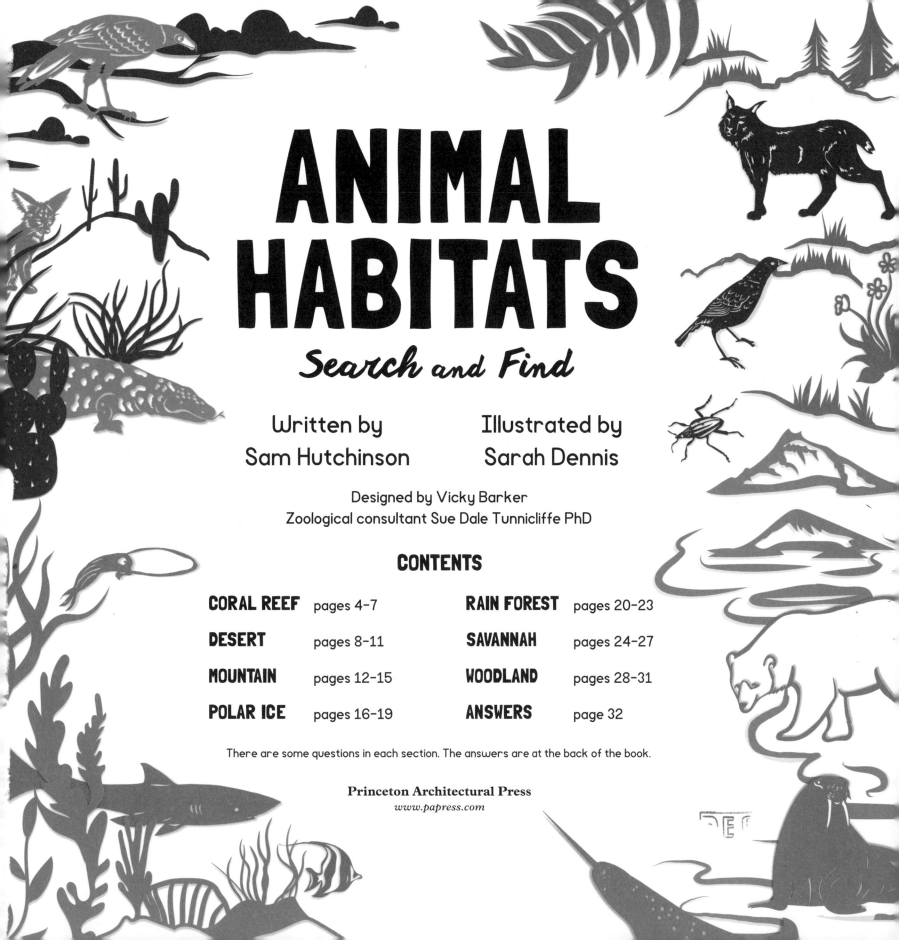

# ANIMAL HABITATS
## *Search and Find*

Written by
Sam Hutchinson

Illustrated by
Sarah Dennis

Designed by Vicky Barker
Zoological consultant Sue Dale Tunnicliffe PhD

## CONTENTS

There are some questions in each section. The answers are at the back of the book.

**Princeton Architectural Press**
*www.papress.com*

# FOOD CHAINS AND HABITATS

Plants are living things that create their food from the air and water around them. They do this using energy from the sun. Animals cannot make their own food so they must eat plants or other animals to get their energy. In this way, food is like little packets of energy.

The journey that the energy takes from the sun to plants to animals is called a food chain. Each step traces the energy from the sun all the way to the biggest predator at the top of the chain. Food chains differ wildly depending on the habitat, and each habitat contains a complex food web of interlinking chains.

### FOOD CHAIN
a diagram that shows how energy moves from one living thing to another

### PREDATOR
an animal that hunts, captures, and eats other animals

### FOOD WEB
a system of food chains that overlap and rely on each other

### PREY
an animal that is food for another animal

### ENERGY FLOW
the transfer of energy from one link in the food chain to the next

### APEX PREDATOR
an animal that has no predators

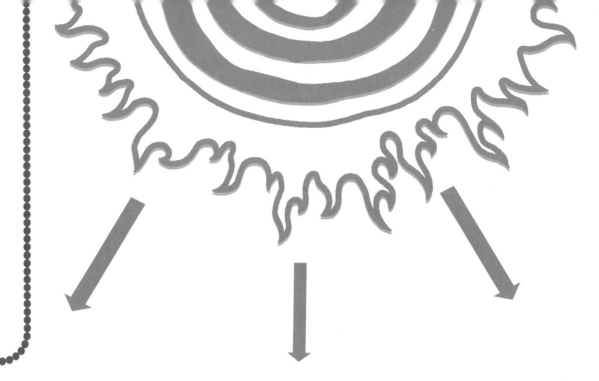

## TROPHIC LEVELS

Each living thing has a place in the food chain that is defined as its trophic level. Every food chain has at least two or three trophic levels and occasionally up to five. Many animals feed at more than one trophic level.

**ENERGY FLOW**

**PRODUCER**
1st trophic level

→ a living thing that makes its own food

**PRIMARY CONSUMER**
2nd trophic level

→ a living thing that feeds on producers

**SECONDARY CONSUMER**
3rd trophic level

→ a living thing that feeds on primary consumers

**TERTIARY CONSUMER**
4th trophic level

→ a living thing that feeds on primary and secondary consumers

**DECOMPOSER**

gets energy from rotting animal or plant matter

Many tertiary consumers eat primary consumers as well as secondary consumers. The food chains in this book group the secondary and tertiary consumers together to show that, when hungry, most creatures will eat whatever they can catch.

3

# A CORAL REEF

Coral is a living creature in the same family as jellyfish and the sea anemone. Its soft, sac-like body grows an exoskeleton (bones on the outside) as protection. After the coral dies, another coral will settle on top. Over time, they build a dazzling forest of exosekeletons on the sea floor, called a reef.

**Follow the sun's energy along these food chains. There are many more possible ways to link these creatures.**

sea sponge

shrimp

plankton

coral

marine algae

parrotfish

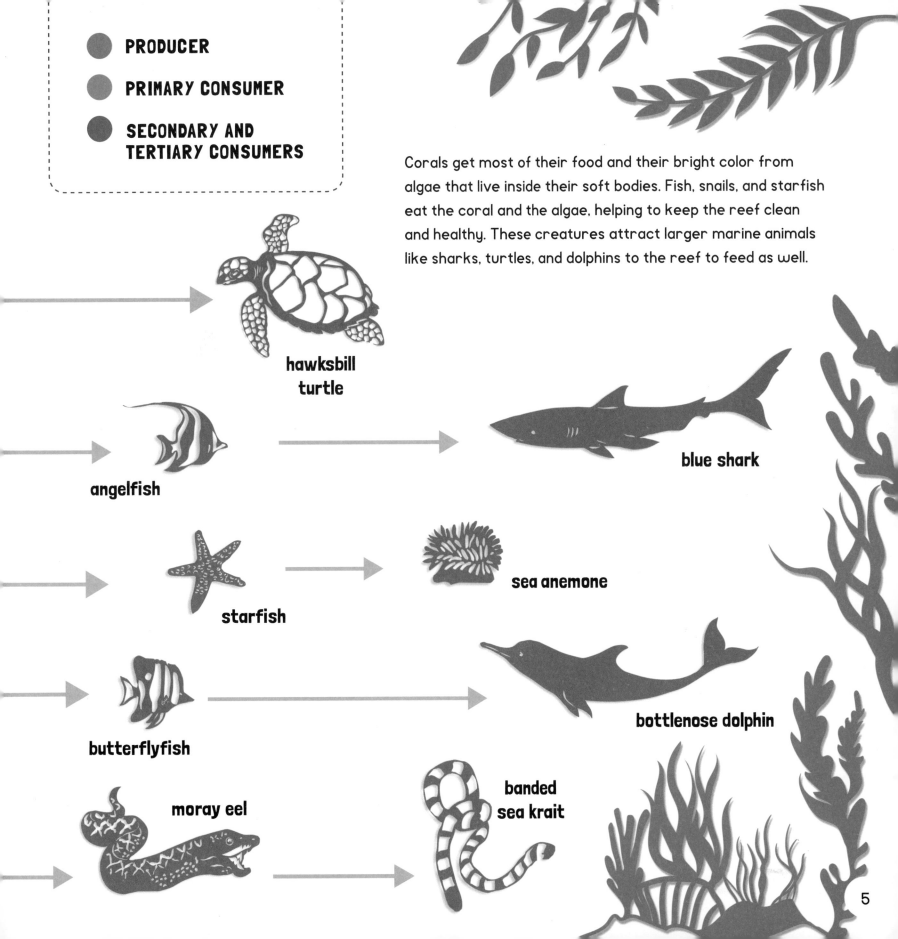

PRODUCER

PRIMARY CONSUMER

SECONDARY AND
TERTIARY CONSUMERS

Corals get most of their food and their bright color from algae that live inside their soft bodies. Fish, snails, and starfish eat the coral and the algae, helping to keep the reef clean and healthy. These creatures attract larger marine animals like sharks, turtles, and dolphins to the reef to feed as well.

hawksbill
turtle

angelfish

blue shark

starfish

sea anemone

butterflyfish

bottlenose dolphin

moray eel

banded
sea krait

5

# FROM CORALS TO SHARKS

Find the producers and consumers in the scene opposite.
What would happen if the plankton disappeared?

## PRODUCERS

marine algae

plankton

## PRIMARY CONSUMERS

shrimp

coral

parrotfish

angelfish

sea sponge

hawksbill turtle

moray eel

## SECONDARY AND TERTIARY CONSUMERS

bottlenose dolphin

banded sea krait

blue shark

sea anemone

starfish

butterflyfish

# DESERT FOOD CHAINS

Deserts are dry areas of land that receive less than 10 in. (25 cm) of rain each year. They are often in very hot parts of the world, but there are also some cold deserts in the polar regions. There are hardly any trees or plants to provide shelter for animals from the scorching midday sun or the extreme drop in temperature when the sun goes down.

Follow the sun's energy along these food chains. Some creatures appear more than once. There are many more possible ways to link these creatures.

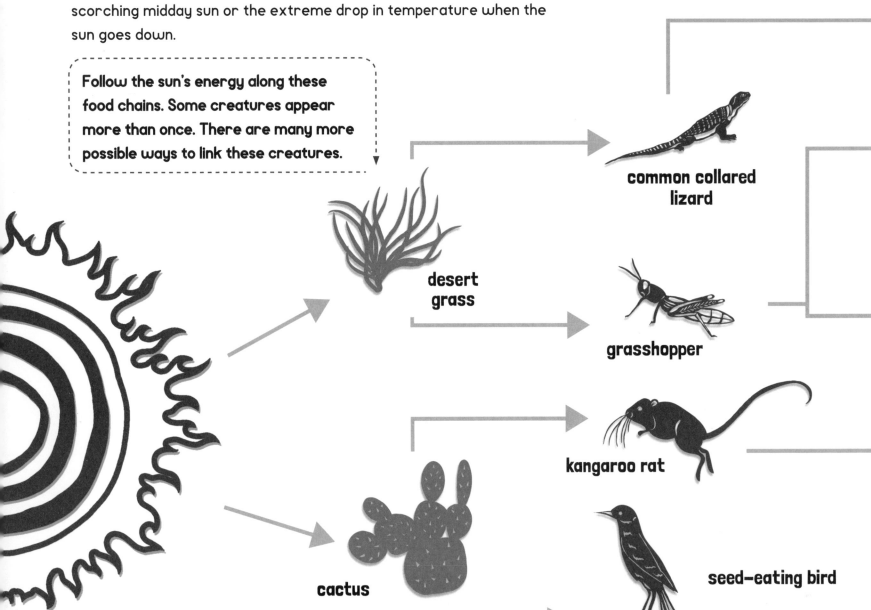

desert grass

common collared lizard

grasshopper

kangaroo rat

cactus

seed-eating bird

Creatures making their home in the desert survive for a long time without water. The catcus stores water in its body for future use and has sharp spines to protect itself. Seeds and flowers from the cactus nourish many insects and small rodents. Lizards and snakes hunt these smaller animals, and they are also prey for hawks and foxes.

gila monster

insect-eating bird

hawk

scorpion

tarantula

fennec fox

hawk

hawk

# A DESERT LANDSCAPE

Find the producers and consumers in the scene opposite.
Which creature is the apex predator?

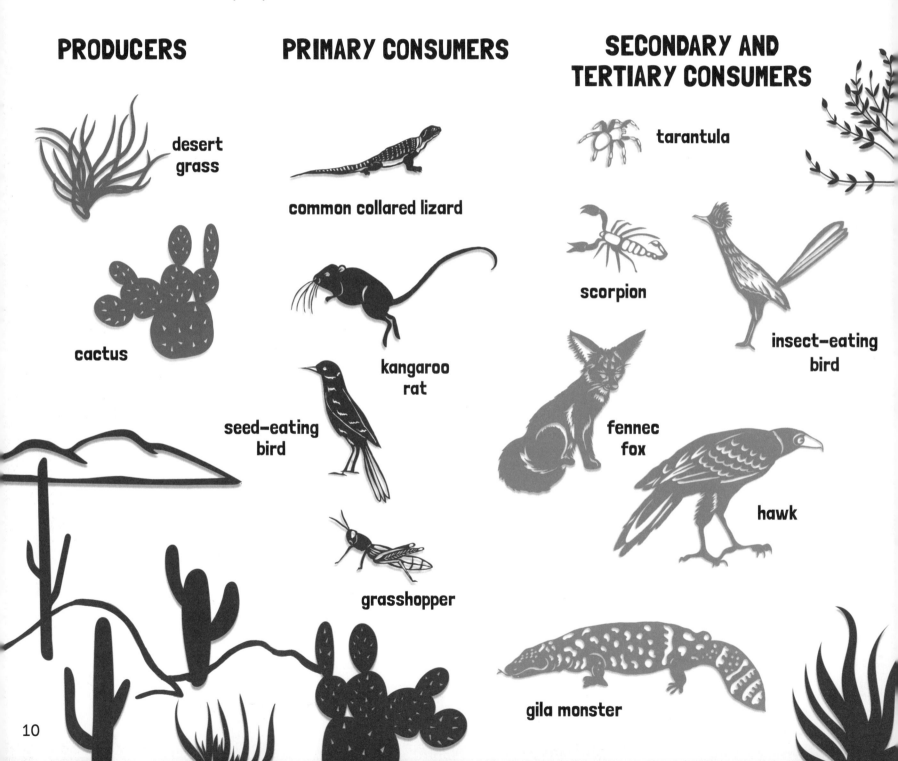

**PRODUCERS**

desert grass

cactus

**PRIMARY CONSUMERS**

common collared lizard

kangaroo rat

seed-eating bird

grasshopper

**SECONDARY AND TERTIARY CONSUMERS**

tarantula

scorpion

insect-eating bird

fennec fox

hawk

gila monster

# MOUNTAIN FOOD CHAINS

Plants, flowers, and pine trees thrive on the mountainside, where there is plenty of water and there are equal amounts of sunshine and shade. These plants are food or shelter for a select number of clever animals who have adapted to living on rocky slopes.

Follow the sun's energy along these food chains. Some creatures appear more than once. There are many more possible ways to link these creatures.

**chamois or ibex**

**plants and flowers**

**insect**

**brown hare**

**red squirrel**

**seeds and nuts**

**marmot**

Predators like the lynx or the eagle owl are able to survive in the cold mountain climate. They have the speed and precision to prey on small animals like the squirrel or hare and the strength to tackle larger animals like the ibex or the chamois.

**lynx**

**alpine accentor**

**eagle owl**

**lynx**

**pine marten**

**eagle owl**

**lynx**

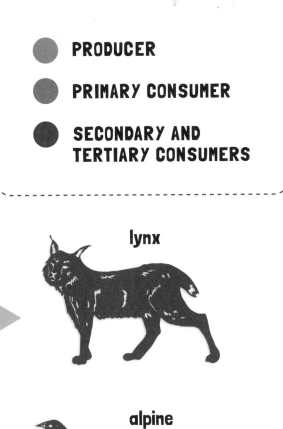

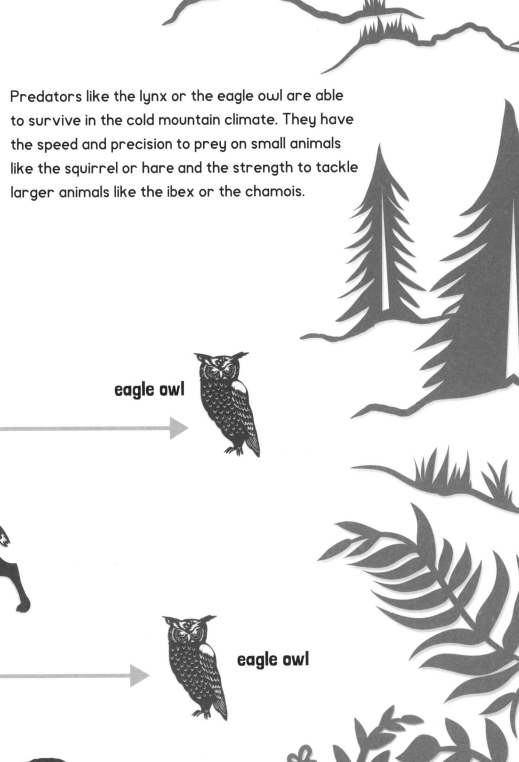

# ON THE MOUNTAIN SLOPES

Find the producers and consumers in the scene opposite.
Are there more primary or more secondary consumers?

## PRODUCERS

plants and flowers

seeds and nuts

## PRIMARY CONSUMERS

ibex

insect

red
squirrel

brown hare

chamois

marmot

## SECONDARY AND
## TERTIARY CONSUMERS

alpine accentor

pine marten

lynx

eagle owl

# POLAR FOOD CHAINS

The frozen Arctic Ocean in the Northern Hemisphere experiences a fascinating double life. In the summer, the sun never sets, melting some of the sea ice and exposing the ocean below to constant sunlight. This increases the growth of algae and phytoplankton, which means there is a huge amount of food to eat!

Follow the sun's energy along these food chains. Some creatures appear more than once. There are many more possible ways to link these creatures.

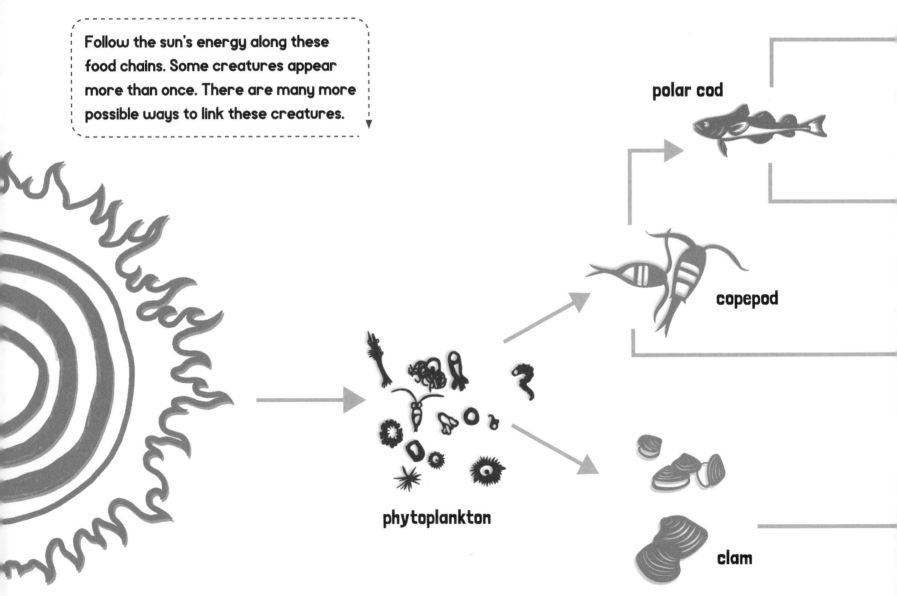

polar cod

copepod

phytoplankton

clam

16

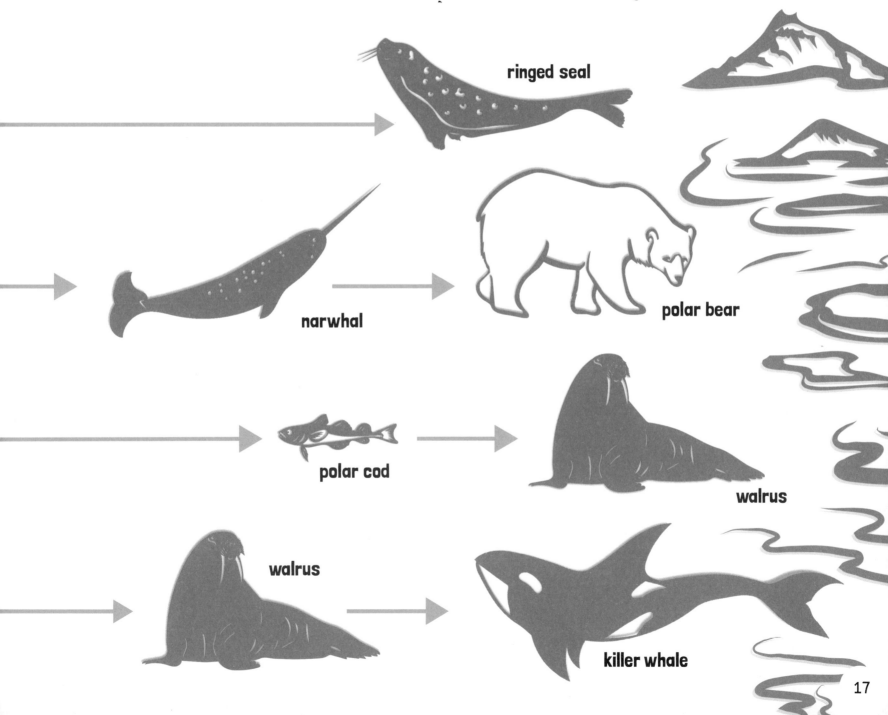

PRODUCER

PRIMARY CONSUMER

SECONDARY AND
TERTIARY CONSUMERS

In October the sun sets and does not rise again until March. The temperature drops, and the ocean freezes over, returning the water below to total darkness. Without sunlight the algae and the phytoplankton cannot grow. Removing the primary producer means every other animal in the food web struggles to find enough to eat. Some animals hibernate, and others migrate.

ringed seal

narwhal

polar bear

polar cod

walrus

walrus

killer whale

17

# LAND OF THE MIDNIGHT SUN

Find the producers and consumers in the scene opposite.
How many of these animals live on top of the sea ice?

## PRODUCERS

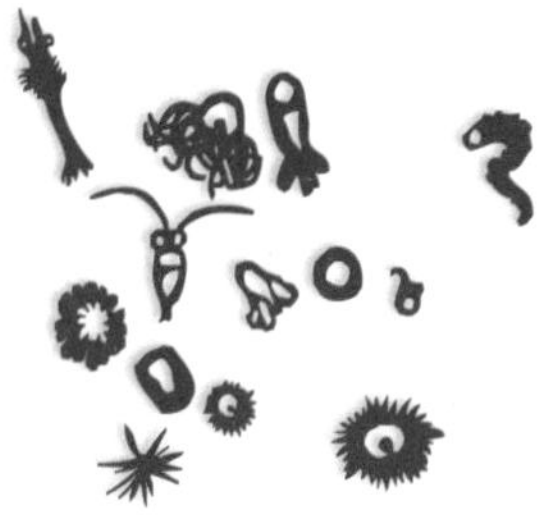

phytoplankton

## PRIMARY CONSUMERS

copepod

clam

## SECONDARY AND TERTIARY CONSUMERS

polar cod

polar bear

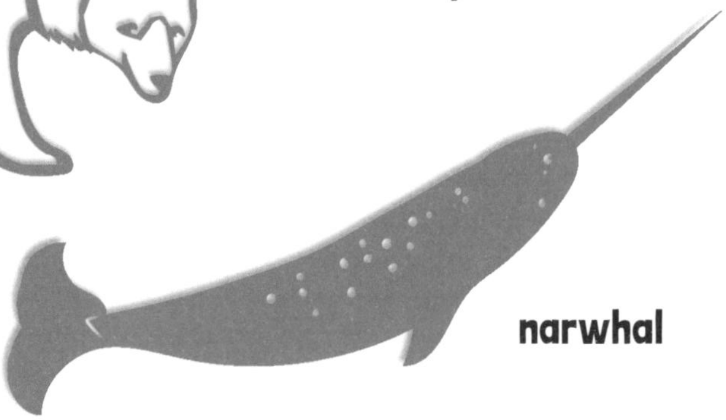

narwhal

ringed seal

killer whale

walrus

# RAIN FOREST FOOD CHAINS

The layers in the trees of a rain forest are full of food for all types of animals. From the many types of fruit trees and flowering plants to insects, mammals of all sizes, birds, snakes, reptiles, fish, and even crocodile-like caimans, the competition is fierce, and most creatures have developed deadly ways of making sure they do not miss out on a meal.

Follow the sun's energy along these food chains. Some creatures appear more than once. There are many more possible ways to link these creatures.

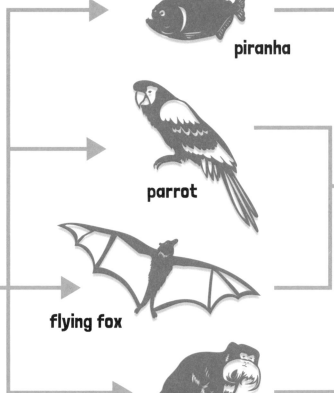

piranha

parrot

flying fox

tamarin monkey

fruit tree

flowering plant

insect

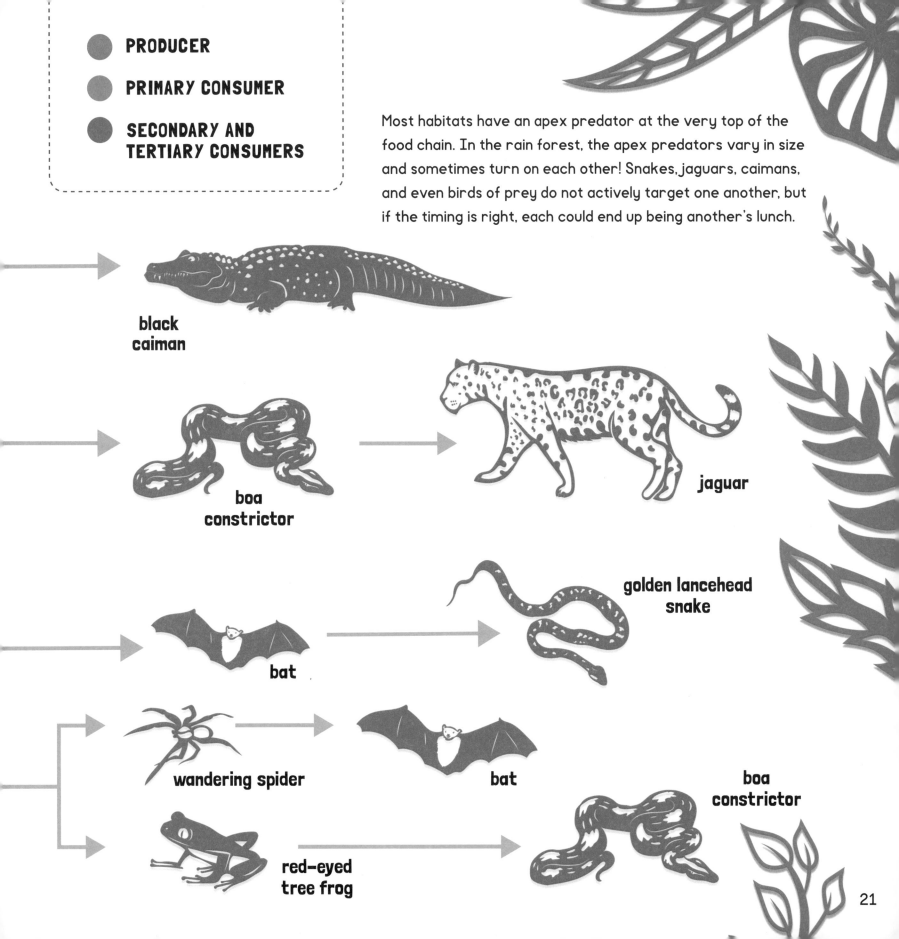

PRODUCER

PRIMARY CONSUMER

SECONDARY AND
TERTIARY CONSUMERS

Most habitats have an apex predator at the very top of the food chain. In the rain forest, the apex predators vary in size and sometimes turn on each other! Snakes, jaguars, caimans, and even birds of prey do not actively target one another, but if the timing is right, each could end up being another's lunch.

black caiman

boa constrictor

jaguar

bat

golden lancehead snake

wandering spider

bat

boa constrictor

red-eyed tree frog

21

# RAIN FOREST TREE CANOPY

Find the producers and consumers in the scene opposite.
Which of these organisms will always sit on the first trophic level of a food chain?

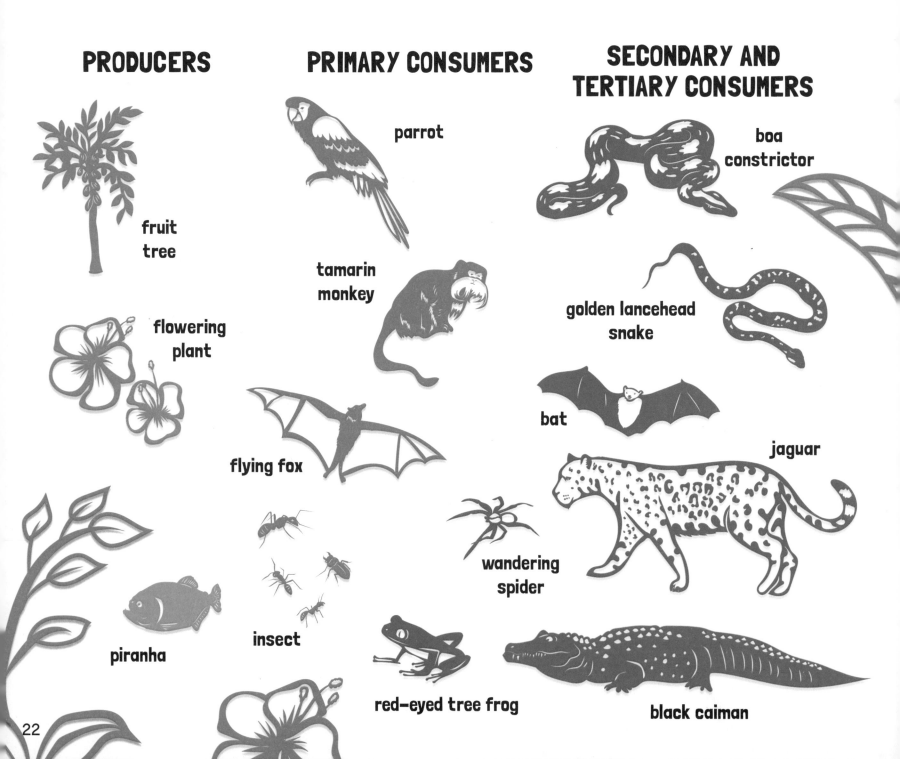

**PRODUCERS**

fruit tree

flowering plant

**PRIMARY CONSUMERS**

parrot

tamarin monkey

flying fox

insect

piranha

red-eyed tree frog

**SECONDARY AND TERTIARY CONSUMERS**

boa constrictor

golden lancehead snake

bat

jaguar

wandering spider

black caiman

22

# SAVANNAH FOOD CHAINS

A rolling, grassy plain full of single trees far enough apart from each other not to touch is called a savannah. During the winter months, the climate is very dry and the landscape is at risk of wildfires. But the summer brings heavy rain and hot, humid temperatures.

Follow the sun's energy along these food chains. There are many more possible ways to link these creatures.

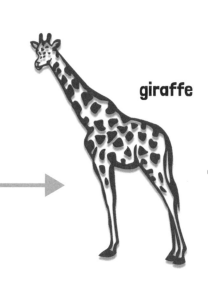

giraffe

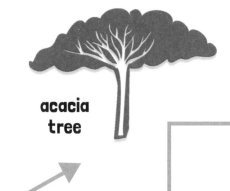

acacia tree

wildebeest

grass

zebra

baboon

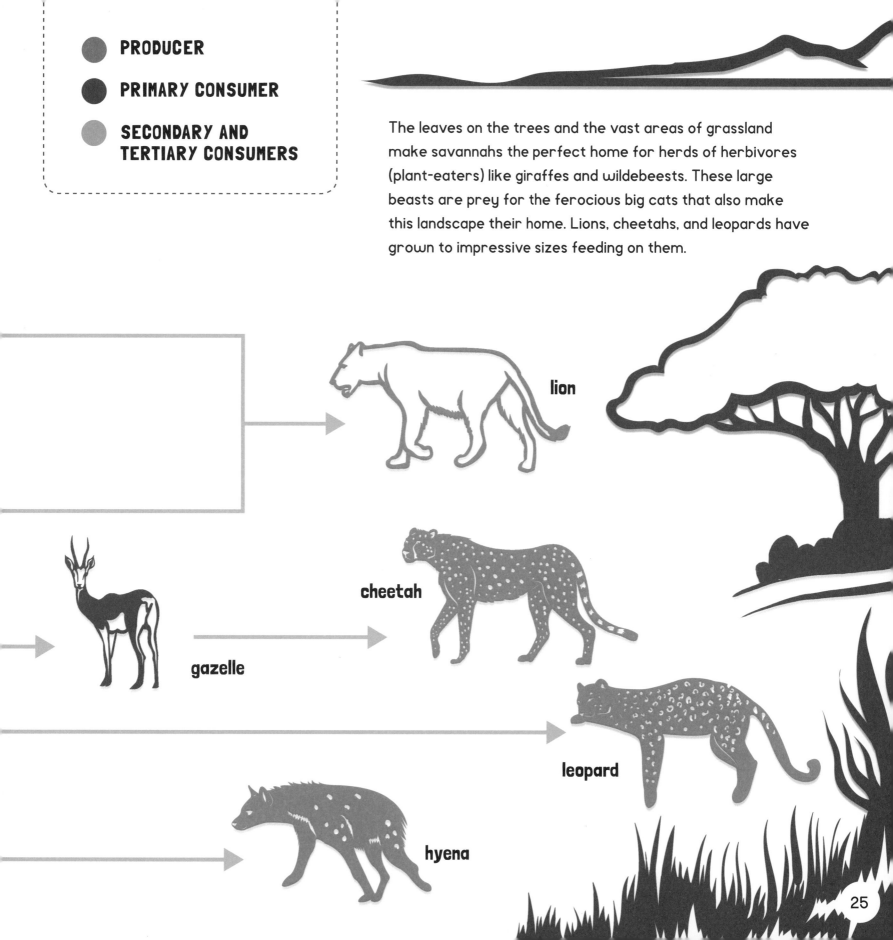

**PRODUCER**

**PRIMARY CONSUMER**

**SECONDARY AND TERTIARY CONSUMERS**

The leaves on the trees and the vast areas of grassland make savannahs the perfect home for herds of herbivores (plant-eaters) like giraffes and wildebeests. These large beasts are prey for the ferocious big cats that also make this landscape their home. Lions, cheetahs, and leopards have grown to impressive sizes feeding on them.

**lion**

**gazelle**

**cheetah**

**leopard**

**hyena**

25

# BIG PREDATORS, BIGGER PREY

Find the producers and consumers in the scene opposite.
Which prey and predator pair is the most different in size?

## PRODUCERS

**acacia tree**

**grass**

**zebra**

**wildebeest**

## PRIMARY CONSUMERS

**giraffe**

**gazelle**

**baboon**

## SECONDARY AND TERTIARY CONSUMERS

**hyena**

**cheetah**

**lion**

**leopard**

# WOODLAND FOOD CHAINS

A gentle landscape of trees, flowers, plants, and grass, called a woodland, is common in parts of the world that have mild climates with plenty of both rainfall and sunshine. The trees are close enough to each other to form a loose canopy, with lots of holes through which the sunlight can reach the ground below.

Follow the sun's energy along these food chains. Some creatures appear more than once. There are many more possible ways to link these creatures.

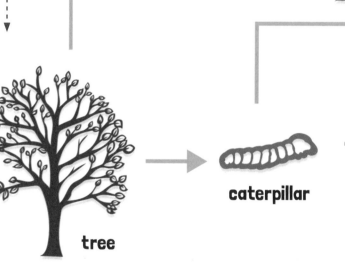

**snail**

**tree**

**caterpillar**

**squirrel**

**fungus**

**earthworm**

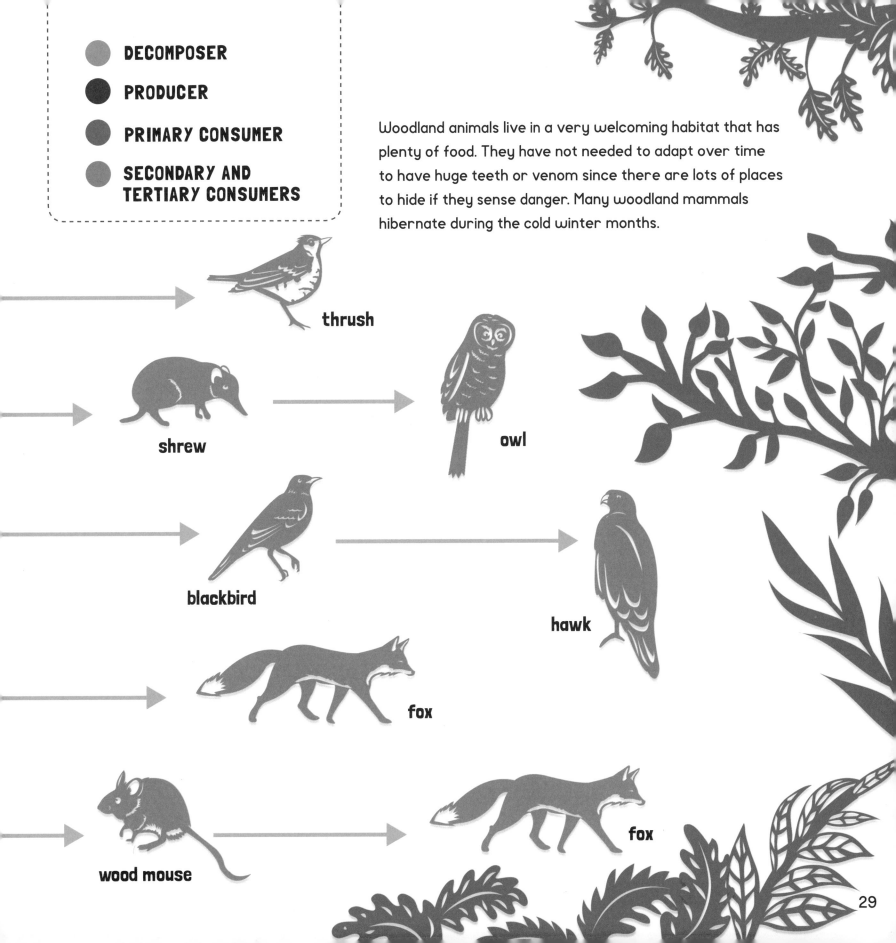

DECOMPOSER

PRODUCER

PRIMARY CONSUMER

SECONDARY AND
TERTIARY CONSUMERS

Woodland animals live in a very welcoming habitat that has plenty of food. They have not needed to adapt over time to have huge teeth or venom since there are lots of places to hide if they sense danger. Many woodland mammals hibernate during the cold winter months.

thrush

shrew

owl

blackbird

hawk

fox

wood mouse

fox

# DANGER FROM ABOVE

Find the producers and consumers in the scene opposite.
How many of these woodland creatures can climb trees?

## PRODUCERS

tree

## PRIMARY CONSUMERS

earthworm

 caterpillar

squirrel

## SECONDARY AND TERTIARY CONSUMERS

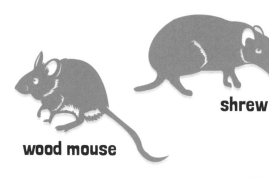

wood mouse

shrew

## DECOMPOSERS

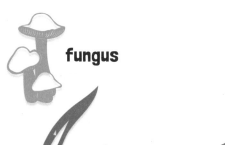

fungus

snail

owl

blackbird

thrush

hawk

fox